formula

the secret to a better life

summersdale

Summersdale Publishers Ltd
46 West Street
Chichester
West Sussex
PO19 1RP
UK

www.summersdale.com

Printed and bound in Great Britain

ISBN 1 84024 510 7

This text came to me after experiencing a spiritual epiphany, so I would like to dedicate this book with thanks to God.

Also, big love to my beautiful wife Sharon.

About the Author

Geoff Thompson is a BAFTA award-winning film maker and one of the UK's most respected martial artists. A prolific writer, he has over a quarter of a million books in print, including his autobiographical bestseller about his days as a nightclub doorman, *Watch my Back*.

Contents

'*Whatever you can do, or dream you can, begin it. Boldness has genius, power, and magic in it. Begin it now.*'

Goethe

Introduction

I find it very exciting that we as a species can be whatever we set our hearts on being and do whatever it is we aim to do; all we need is the right formula.

Introduction

I believe our journey through life is one of self-realisation. By choosing to follow our vocation, the right path for us, we develop our consciousness and find out who we are. We also find out where we are in the whole scope of things and where we can be if we back our dreams with faith and a strong work ethic. Have a look at where you are right now in your life. Now look at where you would like to be and ask yourself why you are not there, or at least on the way there.

the
formula

When I was younger, I worked as a factory floor sweeper. Back then I never imagined that I could make a living out of writing, or that I'd even win awards for it. When I asked myself how I got from that factory floor to where I am today, what choices did I make, what actions did I take that made the journey possible, I stumbled upon a formula. The most important aspect of this formula was that when I stopped trying to help myself and when I focused on other people, that was when I moved forward.

Introduction

What I discovered, and what I will explain within the pages of this book, is that shifting your perspective in this way is a fundamental step towards working out your personal direction in life. This formula shows that you can't simply wish for something and expect it to manifest in front of your very eyes.

the
formula

I believe that there is nothing in life that we cannot achieve, nothing that we cannot have, no one that we cannot become. There is no corner of the world that we cannot access, no fear too large to overcome, no obstacle too great to get round. We just need the right formula. It's a simple one and, while living by it will involve a lot of hard work, it will prove very rewarding.

DESTINATION

the
formula

Think of life as going on a journey. Before you set out in the car you need to know where it is you are going and how you are going to get there. Otherwise you'll drive around blind, wasting fuel. Once your route has been determined you need to make sure that you have plenty of petrol in the tank – in other words, energy – to get you to your destination (or to the first filling station, anyway). After you sort this out, you are on your way.

Destination

As children, most of us knew what we wanted to be when we grew up, but somewhere between childhood and adulthood we had it knocked out of us because 'people like us' don't become astronauts, actors or sculptors. What we know to be true as children often becomes fantasy when we grow up and take the factory job just like our mums, dads, brothers and sisters did.

I was no different: I always wanted to be a writer but allowed people to tell me that this was a silly notion and that I should get myself a proper job and be very grateful for the fact that I had it.

Destination

I believe we are creators. We are able to achieve the most amazing and miraculous things. It is down to us; if we want it, we can have it. Our Creator gave us the gift of free will, to choose to go this way or that, upwards or downwards, to the left or to the right, for good or for bad.

It is our job to set the goals – we have to think, talk and walk them. If we can do these things then we are already halfway there. But this involves effort, discipline and pain, and many of us do not want to experience the discomfort these bring. So we blame others for getting in the way, placing the burden for success and failure on external forces. In doing this we disengage our potential to create.

Destination

I have an objective in life so I channel all of my energy into it. But what if you don't know where you're going, who you want to be or what you wish to achieve? Surround yourself with people who know where they are going and that enthusiasm will rub off. All this will widen your consciousness and give you a different view of the world in which we live.

The more knowledge you acquire the more the world will open up to you.

Eventually your goal, your vocation, will present itself.

For many people their vocation is right in front of them but they fail to accept or recognise it.

Destination

A friend who was a brilliant, potentially world-class judo player complained that he could not find his vocation in life, that he had no direction. I said, 'What about your judo?'

He shrugged his shoulders. 'That's just a hobby, it's just something I do.'

I was in awe watching him perform his hobby. It made me want to be better at what I did, and I was sure it could inspire countless more to achieve greatness in their own vocations. But to him, judo was just recreation, not something he could make a living from or help others with. His vocation was right under his nose – he just failed to see it.

Destination

Others may have the potential to be great artists, writers, motivational speakers, mothers, fathers or carers, but cannot accept – usually due to a common fear of the unknown – that this could be the right thing for them. Ask yourself what it is that you want. You have all the answers though often they will not come until you are ready to hear them.

Focusing on others in my life made me realise how important it is to choose a life goal that also benefits other people. This doesn't mean you have to rush off and save a small village in a Third World country, it means aiming for something that will have some meaning for other people, instead of only helping you. A vocation that is for the good of others might sound very limiting. It isn't. Nearly every profession I can think of serves others in one way or another.

Destination

Your life goal might be to become a **teacher** – think of how many lives you could touch, how many people you could help by simply following your dream.

If your ambition is to **write a screenplay** you should consider how the words and images you create have the potential to help others see the world in a different way.

You might want to become a **professional footballer** but what you may not realise is that when you net the goal that wins the match, you inspire many others on their own paths to greatness.

People, when all's said and done, are the most important things in our lives. Whatever your vocation, don't be in it for the money or the fame because, believe me, these things are transient.

Material wealth is no measure of success and happiness. This is not to say that we should not strive for it; there is no shame in having money or possessions. But don't be fooled into thinking 'If only I had more money, everything would be OK.' If you are not fundamentally happy before gaining riches you will not be any different afterwards.

This doesn't mean you should hide from material wealth or allow it to make you feel guilty. You are not suddenly responsible for the starving children of the world because you are in the black.

Destination

There are many kinds of currency, or resources, and cash is just one of them. It is how we treat cash that determines its worth, not the cash itself. Yet it is true that there is a great responsibility that goes hand-in-hand with having money and it must be treated wisely. People who run away from that obligation are no closer to their destination than those who worship money.

Use the money you have to help you to achieve your goals. It's not helpful to waste a lot of energy worrying about the weekly bills. When our bank balance is healthy we can concentrate less on surviving the next rent increase and more on placing all our energy into our life ambition.

POWERING
THE JOURNEY

To get to our destination we need energy. Energy comes from several things, including the food we eat, the air we breathe and our influences. Let's look at each of these in turn.

The food we eat

I believe that good food adds a spring to the tired feet of good intention. It's easy to miss the connection between our eating habits and our ambitions, but it's important to realise that we can only get out what we put in. If we fill up with dietary rubbish then our performance will reflect that.

To use my earlier analogy, if life is a journey then the body is the car window through which we see the world, so it is essential that we keep it in good order. Maintaining a good diet can be hard but if you want to take this vehicle further than a Sunday afternoon jaunt, you must treat it well and only put in the very best fuel.

Powering the Journey

There are endless food options available these days, many of them processed and full of preservatives, but imagine if we, like our ancestors, were forced to live off the land; no shops or supermarkets, no takeaways. What would we eat? That's the kind of food you should have as your dietary mainstay.

This doesn't mean that you can't have a treat now and then or that you have to live like a monk, only that you should include more healthy options in your diet, such as fruits and vegetables and plenty of fresh water.

Physical training of some sort is also very beneficial if we want our bodies to work at peak proficiency. A lot of our energy can be wasted in a body that is jammed with residual stress hormones. Training flushes them out of your system, clearing the pipes so your thinking isn't clouded. You don't have to become a world-class athlete to see the difference – just get in some good physical workouts every other day.

The air we breathe

When we inhale fresh air the lungs get bumped up to first class status. It is difficult, though not impossible, to choose the air we breathe because it tends to come with the environment in which we live. Yet, as with food, it is what we take in that determines what we get out.

Ideally, if the environment in which you live is full of bad air, and if finances allow, you should change your environment so that the air is better. If this is not possible try and take regular breaks to somewhere that offers good, clean air.

the **formula**

Every four to six weeks I get away to Sherwood Forest for a few days just to top up on fresh, unpolluted air. If you don't like woodland areas, try a holiday by the sea to rejuvenate and empower you. If you think that the air we breathe doesn't affect who and what we are then you should try one of these breaks and see what a profound difference it makes. The first time I took a four-day break to the Forest I felt revitalised for months afterwards.

Powering the
Journey

On a more immediate level try to avoid smoke-filled places like pubs, clubs and bars where all you do is take rubbish into your lungs. Don't tolerate others smoking around you if it is within your power to stop them.

Our influences

This is the biggie, really. More energy is created or stolen by the influences that we allow into our lives than anything else. These influences can be broken down into different categories:

Our immediate environment

You might not realise it but our immediate environment (where we actually live) is responsible for a lot of our energy. Being surrounded by grey walls and uninspiring locales can dampen your spirits, so spruce up the rooms you live in and, if you can, the place in which you work.

My home is always brightly decorated, great music can be heard playing in the background and I have fascinating books by incredible people in nearly every room. I try to make everything around me positive and inspiring – I've even plastered the dashboard of my car with inspiring quotations (to read in traffic jams only!) and put magazines with positive articles in the bathroom.

However, don't blame your environment for your failures. So many people use their environment as a scapegoat for their shortcomings. 'If it wasn't for where I lived I could really do something with my life,' is a common complaint. If you are not happy with your environment then change it. You have the ability to do this.

If people used as much energy
seeking solutions as they did on belly-
aching about how cruel the world is,
their lives would be more complete.

If you can't move to a better
environment immediately then
change the one that you have for
the better until you can. If you are
truly stuck, it's still not a reason to
throw in the towel.

Remember, some of the greatest men and women in history developed their genius in terrible environments:

Powering the Journey

Viktor Frankl wrote his master-piece *Man's Search For Meaning* on scraps of paper in a German death camp during the Second World War.

Billy Connolly was brought up in the rough tenement blocks of Glasgow, but went on to achieve global fame as both a comedian and an actor.

Oprah Winfrey was raised in abject poverty and didn't receive her first pair of shoes until she was six years old, yet she is now one of the most successful and wealthy businesswomen of the twenty-first century.

They all made the very best of what they had. Make sure that you make the very best of what *you* have.

Our friends and family

Negative people can steal a lot of our energy – but only if we let them. You can be feeling on top of the world when, out of the blue, someone says something negative and steals the wind right out of your sails.

the
formula

One of my friends, a very positive young man, told me that he often comes down for breakfast in the morning feeling ready for a productive day. He feels as though nothing can dampen his spirits until his mother says, 'What hare-brained scheme are you chasing today?' And it flattens him like a shadow, so much so that he thinks, 'What's the point of it all?'

They say that you can choose your friends but you can't choose your family. This is true, of course, but you can choose how you allow them to speak to you.

Most people do not realise the power of their words so it is up to you to encourage your family and friends to be more supportive so that they can help and not hinder your aspirations.

Powering the Journey

If you just sit there and take whatever is slung at you, then people will disrespect you all day long. If, however, we stop the rot and say, 'Actually, I'm not having this any more,' then the chances are they'll stop.

What we must remember is that we are each part of our families' and friends' comfort zones, so if you start to move from or expand those comfort zones it will affect those around you. It will leave a vacuum in their lives and they'll feel uncomfortable. Their way of coping with this is to drag you back into their comfort zone by criticising your decisions. Don't have any of it. Ask for support or move on.

Our friends are often worse than our family because they feel abandoned when we 'move up'. If you think enough of them you'll try and take them with you, though this can prove very difficult. People cannot be made to grow; they have to want and earn it.

Explain to a critical friend that you don't like their negative attitude and that they are holding you back. Ask them to change. If you've tried your best and they are still not supporting you, then it's not your fault. When it's their turn to go after their ambitions, try to be there for them. Until that time comes, move on.

I can't tell you how often, as a younger man, I let people pull me down, as though I was duty bound to abandon my aspirations. Who did I think I was, believing I deserved a better life? Friends, or so called, would mock my dreams and leave me feeling bad for days. And the next time we spoke I'd let them do the very same thing again.

I just didn't want the hassle or the embarrassment of speaking my mind. Also, I didn't want to make them feel bad by telling them how they made me feel.

But then I thought about it; they didn't mind making me feel bad so why should I worry about offending them by standing up for myself? Now I have changed totally. I won't have it.

It's unacceptable for anyone to ill-treat you, but remember, you're the one who tolerates it. When you accept this responsibility and do something about it, it'll stop. Negative people will drag you down; they will make you feel as though you cannot achieve anything in life. And once you believe it, it'll become your truth.

This doesn't mean that you should avoid constructive criticism – it's hard to progress if you don't take good advice. Just make sure that the critique is meant to aid your aspirations, not impede them.

Ourselves

We also influence ourselves. When we do something good we feel pleased, and this empowers us and gives us energy. When we let ourselves down we punish ourselves with lowered self-esteem, basically penalising ourselves for our wrongs by taking away energy. With this in mind it is important that we take a long, hard and honest look in the mirror and start to change the things we don't like, or that we think are wrong about ourselves.

Powering the Journey

This can be a difficult task because many of us cannot bear to see the truth. We hide by using unconscious defence mechanisms, rationalising our weaknesses or projecting them onto others. It is only when we accept our weaknesses that we can exorcise them and build strength and integrity.

The soap opera syndrome

Don't allow yourself to get pulled into what I call the 'soap opera syndrome', where a group of people sits around a table gossiping about someone who isn't there, or slagging off someone who cannot defend themselves. This is a big waste of time and energy.

I know it's very easy to get dragged into derogatory conversations, but if we want to achieve great things we have to start by making ourselves great, by rising above the petty jealousies of everyday life.

Re-train yourself to look for the good in each person and each situation. Fill your day with learning and speak only about the good that can be achieved.

Think of energy as currency; every time you use energy for something that is not productive you are throwing money down the drain. Don't waste something that is so precious. If you don't have anything good to say then don't say anything.

Resisting the untrue

In theory this should be an easy one to understand. After all, we know what is right and what is wrong – don't we?

Being wrong is often one of the steps that we take on the way to being right. We believe what we know – in fact, our truth is determined by the information that's available to us, and the more we know the more our truth changes.

That's why I think it's imperative that we get a solid educational foundation (and we are not only educated in a classroom). My only problem is that there are not enough hours in the day to get all the information that I would like! I want my truth to change, I want to know more, but I know that at this moment in time my mind is not big enough to take it all in. Yet it will be.

As a young man, I worked as a nightclub doorman and I used to hit the people I felt were a threat to me. I felt fine about it because at that time I thought I was right, that violence was justifiable. With the information that I had then that was my truth. With the information I have now I know that I was wrong, that I was not justified in much of the violence I carried out.

We must understand that no one is really right or wrong, there are just different levels of truth. Truth is a very subjective matter and we must strive not only to allow our own truth to mature but also to allow others a different truth.

Powering the Journey

One of the ways to gain more energy to help you on your journey is to stop lying to yourself and rationalising behaviour that you know is wrong. Every time you give in to temptation and do the wrong thing, you lose energy and move one step back on your journey. The opposite is also true – every time you do the right thing, you top up on energy.

Be careful because the temptations can often be hidden or vague and there will be plenty of people around trying to convince you to give in, that it'll be OK because 'everyone does it'.

Controlling excitement

Overexcitement runs away with energy and can leave you feeling exhausted.

When I was younger I actually used to make myself ill by getting hyped-up before Christmas and holidays. I used to sit and talk about it all the time and when I wasn't talking I'd be thinking, even dreaming about it. After the event I'd be physically and mentally low. I didn't know then that all my energy was being wasted in anticipation of something that never seemed to live up to the picture that I had painted in my mind.

Powering the Journey

Excitement and stress force the brain into overload and that very small organ then triggers the sympathetic nervous system, quickly using up to half of our oxygen supply, giving us a short-term benefit but wasting masses of energy. Small wonder that overexcitement has us exhausted before the event even unfolds.

It's lovely to look forward to things – just don't allow it to run away with all the fuel that you are going to need when the event arrives. It's a bit like sitting in your car waiting for the lights to change with the gears in neutral and your foot on the accelerator.

Taking time out

It is important to work hard but we need to rest and play too. I find that I get great energy from prayer and meditation. Meditating, for me, involves focusing on a simple mantra and allowing my mind to gain valuable respite.

Each person needs to find their own way of resting, whether it's sitting in silence or taking a long, scented bath. When you find the thing that works for you, sometimes it can be better than actual sleep because it allows the mind to recharge its batteries and to pick up energy from all that is around us.

Powering the Journey

Once we've accumulated energy, it's time to use it to achieve our life goals. Going on a journey means moving out of our comfort zones into the unknown, seeking new pastures to find and realise our goals. I can give you bags and bags of fuel but what use is it if you are too afraid to get in the car and drive?

So the next step is fighting the fear that stops you from getting out onto the road. There are no seasons on this journey, we don't do less because it's a bit cold, or a bit hot, because it's raining, or because the snow is falling. If you want more than everybody else then you need to work harder than everybody else and face the things that others are afraid to face.

Powering the Journey

Per ardua ad astra

(Through hardship to the stars)

If a fear is too big, break it up into smaller, more manageable components. Say, for example, that you've been asked to give a speech at a friend's wedding but speaking in public is your biggest fear. Take it slowly – first, stand in front of a mirror and read your speech aloud. Then ask a friend to listen to you. Gradually build up your confidence until giving your speech in front of the crowd on the big day isn't the terrifying spectacle it once was.

Each time we face a fear and step into adversity our self-esteem grows, and each time we get a success behind us, we become more confident of overcoming the next hurdle. In the end, with a series of successes under our belts, we will understand that there is nothing that we cannot do.

INVESTING
YOUR ENERGY

Helping someone with a good deed is our greatest expression of love... until you sit and tell others what a great person you are because you did the good deed. I'm as guilty as the next man on this score – it's a compelling temptation.

Giving completely freely, without expecting recompense, is hard, but it's something we should learn to do. It should be done because it is right, not because our mates will like us more or will repay the favour.

Giving to others is where most of our energy is generated. You'll find that using your time and skills to help other people will satisfy a natural instinct and give you a kind of 'buzz' that will shake you out of any apathy. When we give it comes back to us tenfold, thus allowing us to give more, creating a self-perpetuating cycle of energy that we can pour into our life goal.

This ultimate ambition can also serve others – remember what I said about teachers. The same can be said for many other professions; it's just a matter of perspective and motivation.

Think of 'giving' as an investment that cannot fail, a bet you cannot lose, an infinite pool of energy that can be dipped into at any time. The more you give the more you get back.

Investing
Your Energy

If it is such a sure bet why don't we give more, why don't we share our energy more often? Probably because most people have forgotten, or possibly not learned, that giving is all that there really is. It is the single most important thing we can do as a species and the only mark we are likely to leave on the world.

Call it karma, call it justice; the beauty of it is that when we serve others we also serve ourselves. So why should we give out rubbish when that is exactly what we will get back?

Investing Your Energy

People who want help are all around us, and they're not so hard to find. Localise your philanthropy. When I told my wife that I wanted to help others but I didn't know where to start, she pointed out that I had ten letters from people who had written to me asking for my help and advice and that I should start there. I was so busy looking for someone to help that I didn't see those who had crossed my path.

the formula

My friend, infused with a giving spirit, told me he wanted to save a rainforest in his bid to help others. Remembering my wife's solid advice to me, I said, 'Why don't you start by helping others directly – your secretary who can't cope with her workload or your daughter who needs your guidance? There are a million people that you can help, and they're all around you – build up to the rainforest.'

To summarise this all-important formula, it begins with you working from the inside out: help yourself first, because if you're not right how can you help others?

Then help those closest to you, your family and friends, slowly extending to those outside the family unit and, depending upon how much you want to achieve, to as many people in the world as you can.

Giving needs to be practised so that it becomes a habit. A book such as this might give you the energy to get the ball rolling, but then you have to keep the momentum going.

Once you do this, the ball will find perpetual motion and roll itself, and you'll have all the energy and direction you need to reach your goal.

I often wonder if people, especially famous people, actually realise the power that one word, one letter or one phone call could mean to someone who holds them in esteem. These people could potentially change the course of millions of lives.

Epilogue

Winston Churchill once said that many people stumble upon the truth and then get back up and walk away as though nothing happened. That's because the truth is often too simple.

Epilogue

I have made this formula my life. With it I've experienced great happiness and I am achieving all the things that I always wanted. I believe I will accomplish all the things that I aim for because I now know the formula.

the
formula

'It is not because things are difficult that
we dare not, it is because we do not dare
that they are difficult.'

Seneca

geoff thompson

shape
shifter

transform your life in 1 day

powerful advice on
personal development

Shape Shifter
Transform Your Life in 1 Day
Geoff Thompson
£7.99 Pb

Powerful advice on personal development from an underdog turned success story.

Do you believe that the world's leading lights are gifted from birth or even just plain lucky? In this groundbreaking guide, **Geoff Thompson** demonstrates that *anyone* with average ability and a strong desire to succeed can do so in any chosen field.

The former bouncer and factory floor sweeper, now a BAFTA award-winning film-maker, author of 30 books, acclaimed screenwriter and martial arts expert, knows this better than most. From Day One, this book will provide inspiration and prove that everyone has the potential to achieve their own personal ambition.

'One of the best new writers to come out of Britain'
Ray Winstone, actor

Chapter One

What is Shape Shifting?

Shape shifting is a tried and tested method of personal transformation. It encourages and nurtures excellence in any chosen field through consistent practice. It employs under-the-bonnet visualisation (which we will look at in a later chapter) as its core, and peer exposure as its sustenance. It has worked for me and I trust without question that it can work for you and for anyone else.

> Most people fail because they simply choose not to succeed. Often that choice is unconscious and the decision fraught with undefined fear.

We all have the ability to change who we are for who we would dearly love to become. This is no idle boast; I have used and perfected this methodology over a number of years. It is what has enabled me to enjoy a charmed life. I spend my mornings writing in my pyjamas and slippers with fresh cups of honey-sweetened tea ever on supply. My afternoons are dedicated to café-trekking with my wife.

I love my life.

It wasn't always that way. Like many people, I once hated the hard graft of my days, working in a job I despised, living a life that brought me little pleasure. It was only the concept of shape shifting, and my ability to adopt it, that enabled me to escape the slavish bonds of societal expectation and live a life more befitting of my wants. A life that I chose to live as opposed to a hand-me-down nine-to-five existence that I neither wanted nor took particular delight in. The process of shape shifting belongs to us all. Since man first walked the Earth, he has transformed himself in the forge that necessity and desire cast. This transformation, however, has usually been unconscious. What

I intend to do within the pages of this book is draw the unconscious process into consciousness, bring it into the light so that its practice and perfection can be better understood and more readily employed.

Anyone with a sure desire for change and a strong work ethic will have the opportunity to realise the very best of their imaginings.

I ask not that you take my word for it, only that you read the book, assess the data, put it to the test and make up your own mind.

geoff thompson

stress buster

how to stop stress
from killing you

Stress Buster
How to Stop Stress from Killing You
Geoff Thompson
£7.99 Pb

This book may save your life.

In our increasingly hectic society we are under constant pressure to get the best results, the top job, a better car or a bigger house. For many reasons, stress can become a major problem affecting our relationships and even our health. Stress can ruin lives, and most people don't know how to cope with it – or how they can use it as an energy force.

If you're always getting angry in the car, at home or at work, if you constantly feel out of balance, then this book is for you. It will help you identify the causes of stress in your life, and shows you how to deal with them in a practical way. With true-life examples, clear explanations and relevant advice, it's an indispensable aid to overcoming stress.

THE ELEPHANT AND THE TWIG

The Art Of Positive Thinking

14 Golden Rules to Success and Happiness

GEOFF THOMPSON

author of *Watch My Back* and *Fear*

SUMMERSDALE

The Elephant and the Twig
The Art of Positive Thinking
Geoff Thompson
£12.99 Hb

Do you ever feel like you are tied to an immovable object and can't break free? That you couldn't possibly give that presentation at work, that you would never be able to go it alone in business, or that you have to remain stuck in a social and lifestyle rut as there is no other alternative? This book shows you that, when it comes down to it, what ties you and prevents you from realising your potential is only a 'twig'. **Geoff Thompson** guides you through the process of breaking the negative thinking that binds us all and helps you to take the plunge and properly take on life.

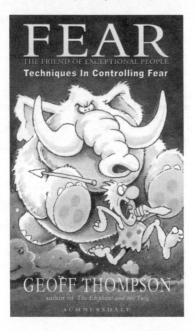

Fear
The Friend of Exceptional People
Geoff Thompson
£12.99 Hb

Once a doorman at some of Britain's roughest nightclubs and now a world-renowned martial artist, **Geoff Thompson** has had more to be frightened of than most. Here he shares his secrets for overcoming your fears to help you live life to the max. From spiders to public speaking, job interviews to physical conflict, Geoff takes you through proven techniques of combating whatever it is you're afraid of.

- Understand your physical reactions to fear and how they can be used to your advantage
- Overcome the negative feelings that make you think you can't succeed
- Learn methods to defeat your fears with Geoff's unique Fear Pyramid system
- Achieve your full potential without worries restricting you Geoff has included interviews with people from the SAS and the boxing circuit to inspire you to believe that nothing should hold you back from living your dreams.

www.summersdale.com